Weird and Wonderful
ANIMAL FACTS

Written by Anne Rooney
Illustrated by Ro Ledesma

ARCTURUS

ARCTURUS

This edition published in 2024 by Arcturus Publishing Limited
26/27 Bickels Yard, 151–153 Bermondsey Street,
London SE1 3HA

Writer: Anne Rooney
Illustrator: Ro Ledesma
Designer: Supriya Sahai
Editors: Lydia Halliday and
 Lucy Doncaster
Managing Editor: Joe Harris
Managing Designer: Rosie Bellwood

ISBN: 978-1-3988-4470-4
CH011578NT
Supplier 29, Date 0624, PI 00006521

Printed in China

Stick your beak into some incredible bird facts on pages 38–39.

Take a deep dive underwater with whale facts on pages 78–79.

YAWN! If mammals are more your speed, check out pages 58–59.

If you get a buzz from insect facts, turn to pages 56–57.

ABOUT THIS BOOK

This weird and wonderful book is packed with absolutely wild facts—all about animals! You'll find out about frogs that freeze but don't die, lizards that spit blood from their eyes, and tiny animals that seem almost indestructible!

You can read this book from beginning to end, or you can flip through until you find something that sounds especially intriguing.

So what are you waiting for? It's time to make like a penguin and plunge right in!

SOME JELLYFISH CAN LIVE FOREVER

Most animals start as babies and end as adults—it's a one-way street. Worms, zebras, ants, porcupines, lizards ... just about everything has a limited lifespan. Except for a few jellyfish. If a *Turritopsis* jellyfish feels its age, it reverts to its baby stage and starts all over again. In theory, it's immortal—though it can die by being eaten.

LIFE STAGES

As a baby, you were just a small human, but not all animals start off looking like their parents—butterflies spend time as caterpillars, and frogs spend time as tadpoles. Jellyfish eggs first form into a planula, which settles on a surface and grows into a polyp. Fixed to a rock or the seabed, it waves its tentacles in the water to trap food. When it's big enough, the polyp makes buds. These grow into jellyfish and separate, swimming off to start life alone.

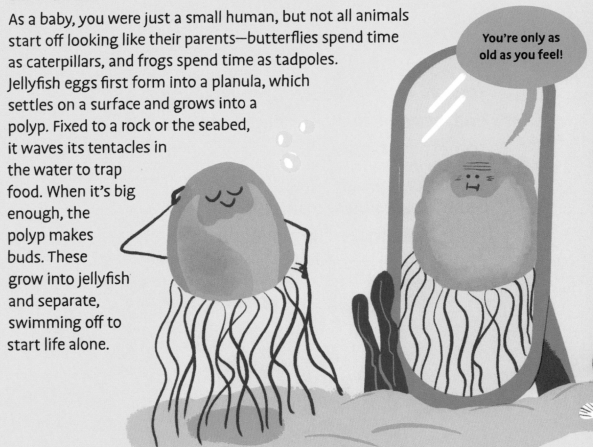

You're only as old as you feel!

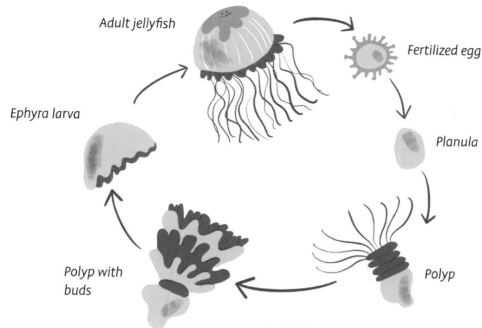

Adult jellyfish

Fertilized egg

Ephyra larva

Planula

Polyp with buds

Polyp

CHANGING CELLS

A fertilized egg (an egg that has been joined by a sperm) starts out with cells of one type that copy themselves to make a new organism (living thing). Humans have different types of cells—blood, bone, muscle, nerve, and others. To make these, cells differentiate (become different). The same happens in a jellyfish. But a jellyfish can also put this process into reverse, called transdifferentiation. It falls to the seabed and turns into a blob, called a cyst, while it turns back into polyp cells. Then it starts the whole cycle all over again!

DANGER!

Jellyfish use transdifferentiation when they're injured, or when living conditions are really bad and they are in mortal danger. This helps them to survive almost anything, except for being eaten!

Fast Facts

Name: *Turritopsis* jellyfish
Size: 5 mm (0.2 in) across
Home: Oceans worldwide
Eats: Plankton, fish eggs, larvae of other sea creatures

SNAILS HAVE TEETH—LOTS OF THEM!

You probably think of slugs and snails as being all soft and squishy, but they're hiding something. A garden snail has about 14,000 teeth! These teeth are tiny (they have to be to fit in a snail's mouth) and are all bunched together in a flexible band called a radula.

TAKING A PEEK

To see a slug's or snail's mouth you need to get underneath it. The best way to do that is to get it to crawl over a pane of glass. Slugs and snails move by making slime, which they drag themselves over. The mouth is at the front (in the head—they're not so weird that they have their mouth somewhere else!) and you might get to see it if you put something on the glass that the slimy beast wants to eat.

SNAIL SNACKS

Slugs and snails are mollusks. Gardeners grumble about them eating their plants, but different types eat lots of different things, including fruit, leaves, worms, decomposing (rotting) dead things, and even other slugs.

Fast Facts

Name: Garden snail
Size: 2.5–4 cm (1–1.6 in) across the shell
Home: Europe, North Africa, western Asia—but there are different types of snails worldwide
Eats: Leaves

A mollusk can bite off a chunk with its single jaw and pass it to its radula to be scraped into small pieces. Or it can just use its radula to scrape food from the surface it's on. Shellfish such as limpets also have a radula and use it to scrape algae or seaweed from rocks. Rock-scraping is hard on the teeth, and they wear out and need replacing. Imagine how your teeth would fare if you had to scrape your food off a rock!

CHAMELEONS USE CRYSTALS FOR CAMOUFLAGE

A chameleon is a type of lizard that mostly lives in Africa. Chameleons are experts at disguise and can change their appearance to blend in with their surroundings at a moment's notice. They can change from green to brown to red to yellow and any pattern they need so they can hide against the background. They do this using lots of nanocrystals (very tiny crystals) inside the skin.

NOW YOU SEE ME ... NOW YOU DON'T!

The shade of a chameleon is determined by the wavelength of light reflected by the nanocrystals. To change its appearance, it shifts the nanocrystals around to reflect light differently.

A relaxed chameleon keeps its nanocrystals close together, so they reflect light of shorter wavelengths, such as blue. Since the chameleon has a bit of yellow pigment in its skin, it looks green, helping it hide against leaves. If it gets stressed, it puffs itself up and the nanocrystals move farther apart, so they reflect light of longer wavelengths. This makes the chameleon look orange or red.

HIDDEN IN PLAIN SIGHT

Animals that are in danger of being eaten, or that want to eat others, often have patterns that help them blend into the background. It's why lions are the browny-yellow of dead grass and polar bears look as white as snow. It's called camouflage. Animals with stripes or splodges, such as zebras and giraffes, use patterns to break up their outlines so that predators (animals that eat them) find it hard to see them against the background or to pick out individual animals in a group. But few animals can change their appearance like the chameleon!

You've really BRIGHTENED up my day!

Fast Facts

Name: Common chameleon
Size: 15–40 cm (6–16 in) long
Home: Africa, southern Europe, southern Asia
Eats: Insects, worms, leaves

A COCKROACH AND ITS HEAD CAN LIVE SEPARATELY

If a cockroach has an accident that involves its head being cut off, it can survive for a few weeks. Eerily, so can the head. The cockroach will eventually die of starvation, though, since it can't eat without a head. The body might also have another accident as it can't see where it's going!

HOW DOES A COCKROACH SURVIVE WITHOUT A HEAD?

A cockroach doesn't pump blood around its body, so it wouldn't keep gushing out after its head was cut off. The blood would soon clot (clump together) and seal the cut. It also doesn't need a brain to control breathing or movement. This is because a cockroach doesn't have lungs. Instead, it has little holes in its body called spiracles, which let in the oxygen it needs. It also has bunches of nerves in sections of its body away from the brain that deal with movement and responding to changes in the surroundings. It can survive for several weeks without food.

Have you seen my body somewhere around here?

WHAT HAPPENS TO THE HEAD?

The head doesn't survive as long without a body as the body does without a head. Even so, it will wave its antennae (feelers on its head) around for a few hours. If the head is kept cold and given nutrients, it survives longer.

EVERY KĀKĀPŌ WEARS A BACKPACK

The kākāpō is a ground-living, flightless parrot found only in New Zealand. Kākāpōs are so endangered that every one now wears a backpack with an electronic tracking device. This tells researchers where each bird is and when it mates. There's no privacy for a modern kākāpō!

HELP WITH THE BABIES

Kākāpōs aren't great at having babies. They lay eggs only once every two to four years and these often don't hatch. Keen to help, researchers take all the eggs from a kākāpō nest and replace them with 3-D printed eggs that fool the parents. Meanwhile, they hatch the chicks in an incubator—a warmed box that is set at just the right temperature. To keep the kākāpō parents happy, the printed eggs have electronics inside and make the same noises as an unhatched chick. When the chicks hatch, scientists quickly slip them into the nest and remove the fake eggs!

WEIRD AND WONDERFUL

Kākāpōs are perfectly suited to the New Zealand forests they call home. They are green, so they blend in with the plants of the forest floor, and they stay absolutely still if they are in danger. Living on the ground and not flying saves lots of energy. For millions of years, this worked well.

But times have changed, and not being able to fly is now a problem. Humans have brought rats and dogs to New Zealand, which kill kākāpōs on the ground. It is too late for the birds to adapt to this new situation—they gave up flying years ago. This is a good example of how an animal that is well adapted to the conditions where it lives can face real danger if things change.

This egg sounds strange!

SEALS ARE MORE CLOSELY RELATED TO BADGERS THAN TO WHALES

Seals and whales are both big blubbery animals with stumpy limbs that spend their time in the sea. You'd think that maybe they're closely related, but they've just developed to look alike and live in the same way. Dugongs and penguins have a similar shape, too.

We are family.

I've got all my badgers with me!

COMING CLOSER

Animals develop bodies and habits that suit the places and ways they live. The step-by-step changes in animals as they adapt to their living conditions is called evolution.

Sometimes animals end up looking similar but from different starting points. This is called convergent evolution. It's why seals (which are related to bears and badgers) look similar to whales (which are related to hippos), dugongs (which are related to elephants), and penguins (which are related to albatrosses).

Sugar gliders and flying squirrels are another example of convergent evolution. Both are small furry animals that glide between trees using flaps of skin between their wings. But both evolved from different animals without skin flaps.

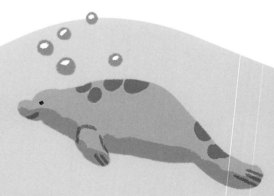

REALLY SIMILAR AND REALLY DIFFERENT

When a feature works well, it often appears more than once. Seals, dugongs, and whales all evolved separately from mammals that lived on land. As their ancestors spent more and more time in the water, so they became more and more streamlined (having an efficient, smooth design). Eventually their limbs became flippers and they came to look fishlike. Penguins are birds, and they've evolved a similar sleek, streamlined shape. They've stopped using their wings to swim and turned them into flippers. They're like a seal with a beak!

ELECTRIC EELS ARE TRULY SHOCKING

Electric eels produce an electric shock to stun prey or drive away predators. Although they're called electric eels, they're not really eels at all, and are more closely related to catfish. They have to breathe air, so they frequently come to the surface of the rivers where they live.

MADE OF BATTERIES

An electric eel's body contains around 6,000 cells that work like miniature batteries, storing electricity. When the eel wants to attack, all the cells discharge (release) their electricity at once, producing a surge great enough to stun and sometimes kill its victim.

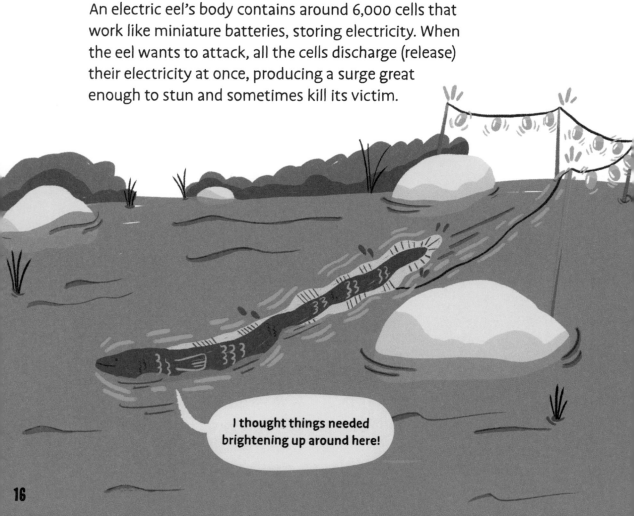

I thought things needed brightening up around here!

Electric eels mostly use their electricity to stun other fish that they want to eat, but they can shock anything that attacks them, too. They also detect (sense) the electricity produced by other animals, using this to find their food in the murky water of muddy rivers. Sometimes they even hunt in packs, herding fish into shallow water and then all zapping them at once.

I'm shocked!

FaSt FactS

Name: Electric eel
Size: Up to 2 m (6 ft 7 in) long
Home: Rivers and swamps in northern South America
Eats: Fish, amphibians, reptiles

FISH OUT OF WATER

The electricity from an activated eel doesn't reach far through the water if the eel isn't touching its target. So, eels sometimes leap out of the water and press their electric bodies against the animal they want to shock. There's even a tale of them attacking horses in this way. By laying its body against the animal, the eel sends the electricity straight into its victim's body, with shocking results.

ANTEATERS ARE VERY ENERGY-EFFICIENT

Anteaters have a very low metabolic rate, though no one knows why. Metabolic rate is the speed at which an animal's body uses energy—in other words, it's a measure of how much energy it uses during a period of time.

ENERGY BUDGETS

Usually, mammals and birds have quite a high metabolic rate since they need to keep their bodies warm. Reptiles and amphibians have a lower metabolic rate since they don't use energy to stay warm. Fish have the lowest metabolic rate. Anteaters keep themselves a bit warm but have the lowest body temperature of any mammal.

ENERGY IN AND ENERGY OUT

An animal gets its energy from food, so an animal with a high metabolic rate needs to eat more than an another the same size with a lower metabolic rate. In case you find yourself needing to look after an anteater, it's useful to know that it needs 350 kilocalories (kcal) a day for each kilogram of body weight. By contrast, a dog needs 460–580 kcal a day per kilogram of body weight. All that energy (for the anteater) has to come from ants! An anteater eats about 35,000 ants each day.

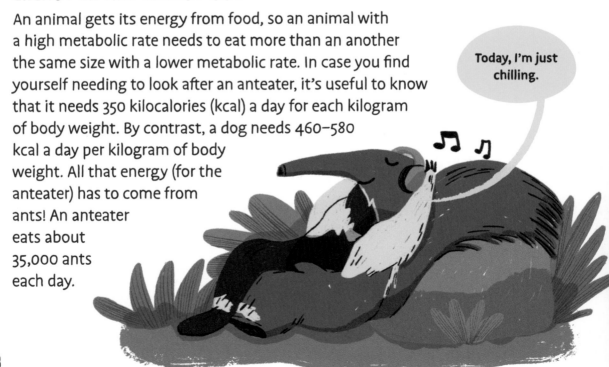

Today, I'm just chilling.

Fast Facts

Name: Giant anteater
Size: Body up to 1.25 m
(4 ft 1 in) long, plus tail
up to 89 cm (35 in) long
Home: Grasslands of Central
America
Eats: Ants, termites

MEASURING METABOLIC RATE

One way of measuring metabolic rate is to work out how much oxygen an animal uses. It needs oxygen for its muscles and brain to work. The more work these do, the more oxygen it needs. When you exercise, you breathe more quickly and your heart beats faster to carry oxygen in your blood to your muscles. Your metabolic rate goes up. When you're not moving about, your metabolic rate is lower. It's the same for other animals. Anteaters don't go to the gym; they spend their day sauntering along eating.

PEACOCKS AREN'T BLUE AND GREEN

Although peacocks look blue, they don't have any chemicals in their feathers that make them blue. Instead, they pull off a neat trick with light, bending it so they look vibrant.

REFLECTION AND REFRACTION

You probably already know that white light can be split into a spectrum or rainbow. If you shine white light through a block of glass or a drop of water, it is split into light of different wavelengths, producing a rainbow. You can shine this rainbow onto a white wall, but no chemical pigments are suddenly present on the wall. Some birds look bright blue, green, or another shade because they have feathers that bounce (reflect) and bend (refract) light in the same way.

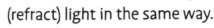

Fast Facts

Name: Blue peafowl (peacock is the name for the male peafowl)
Size: Body 0.9–1.3 m (3 ft–4 ft 3 in) long, plus tail 1.5 m (4 ft 11 in) long (males)
Home: Forests in India
Eats: Plants, seeds, insects, small reptiles, amphibians

REALLY GREEN

One type of bird does have a pigment to make it look green. Turacos live in southern Africa and their feathers are genuinely green, in the usual way that things are green—we can identify a chemical in the feathers that makes them green. This is so unusual, the chemical is named after them—it's called turacoverdin.

Check out my new look!

WHITE PEACOCKS

Some peacocks are entirely white. Their feathers don't do the trick with light to make them look jazzy and sparkly. Interestingly, you can still the pattern of the eye on a white peacock's tail feathers. Looking at a white peacock feather makes it clear that it's the angle and shape of the feather's surface that lies behind the glorious pattern of blue and green.

A STARFISH CAN GROW A NEW ARM...

... and an arm can grow a new starfish! Starfish and brittlestars are star-shaped animals that live in the sea. They have a central body part, where the mouth is, and five or more identical arms that they use to move around.

It's even better than the old one!

The arms are quite easily harmed—they can be bitten off by predators. Luckily, losing an arm doesn't kill the starfish, and it can grow a new one. Even if it loses two or three arms, it will be all right once it's had a chance to replace them.

NEW FOR OLD

Sometimes a predator might eat most of the starfish and leave an arm, or the arm might be broken off in an accident. Amazingly, if the arm has a bit of the central body still attached, the starfish can recreate all of itself from the cells in the body part. It looks odd while its new body grows, since it's one big, long arm with a tiny body to which four smaller arms are attached.

STEMS AND STARS

Living organisms start off as cells that are all the same, called stem cells. As the embryo (pre-baby) grows, the stem cells split, producing more cells. These then differentiate into different types of cells. The starfish has stem cells in the middle part that do this even in an injured adult. So the bit-of-a-starfish can make arm cells, body cells, mouth cells, and so on to rebuild itself.

SLEEPING BATS DON'T FALL DOWN

Bats sleep hanging upside down, clinging to the walls and roofs of caves or high up in trees. They hold on with their feet, and fly by letting go. They don't fall off when they're asleep, or even when they die. This is because tendons in the legs lock in place with their toes gripping on. They need to decide to let go, rather than remember to hold on.

TENDONS, MUSCLES, AND BONES

Your muscles are attached to your bones with tendons (tough bands of fibrous tissue). When a muscle contracts (gets shorter), it pulls on the tendon, and the bone at the other end of the tendon moves toward the contracting muscle.

A bat has talon tendons that connect directly from its toes to its upper body without muscles in between. When the bat wraps its toes around something, it locks the tendons. The weight of its body then holds the toes in the gripping position, until the bat decides to let go.

Fast Facts

Name: Common pipistrelle
Size: Wingspan 18–25 cm (7–10 in)
Home: Europe, northwest Africa,
   parts of Asia
Eats: Flying insects (especially
   gnats, mosquitoes, and midges)

TAKE OFF!

To fly away, a bat needs to use its muscles to lift its body a bit so that the weight is taken off its talon tendons. It can then open its claws, drop into the air, and fly away. That's great if they're hanging upside down, where they should be, but bats can't take off from the ground. So, if for any reason they do fall to the ground, they're stuck.

HORSES WALK ON THEIR MIDDLE TOE

Do you like my new, five-toed look?

The ancestors of horses had five toes. Over millions of years of evolution, horses lost all the other toes and came to walk only on their middle toe.

HOOVES AND NAILS

You might be surprised that horses have toes at all, but a hoof is just a very well-developed toenail. It's made of the same material as your toenails, but is much bigger and thicker, so it's tougher. You can't have a toenail without a toe. If you have one toenail, you need one toe to keep it on!

Fast Facts

Name: Horse
Size: Varies by species; 1.4–1.7 m (4 ft 8 in–5 ft 8 in) tall to the shoulders
Home: Domesticated worldwide; horses first evolved in North America and spread worldwide
Eats: Grass and other low-growing plants

DROPPING TOES

The first horses roamed forests about 56 million years ago. They were tiny, measuring just 50 cm (18 in) from ground to shoulder, and had four toes. As the forests were replaced by grassland, the animals living there adapted. Some hoofed animals (called ungulates) dropped to three toes. Modern examples are rhinos and tapirs. Some settled for two toes, including modern cows, deer, pigs, and sheep.

ON THE HOOF

Some horses evolved long, thin legs with a single toe/hoof about 15 million years ago. These feet were good for running fast over grassland. Horses needed to run fast to escape from large predators that could also run fast. By a million years ago, there were only single-hoofed horses left. But if experts look very closely at the bones of a horse's foot, they can make out the last traces of the other toes.

ALL STARLINGS IN NORTH AMERICA COME FROM 80 RELEASED IN 1890

European starlings are native to Europe, as their name suggests, but there are now about 100 million of them living in North America. How did they get there? It's too far to fly. It turns out that 80 starlings were released in Central Park, New York, in 1890 and 1891 by a man called Eugene Schieffelin. They made themselves at home, started breeding, and were hugely successful. A few had already been brought over and released before this, but Schieffelin's flock was the largest.

TWO, FOUR, SIX ... LOTS!

The starlings did well in North America, adjusting easily to their new home. They can eat a variety of foods and nest in different places. Since starlings lay four to six eggs twice a year, a single pair can soon produce a huge family. They live for two or three years. If a pair produces 12 young in one year, that's up to six new pairs. Each of those pairs, plus the original pair, could produce 12 young the next year, so another 84. That's a total of 96 new starlings from the original pair in just two years!

SPACE INVADERS

People have introduced many animals and plants to areas they couldn't have reached on their own. If they compete successfully with local species, they can take over. They're then called invasive species. Like human invaders, they replace those already living there and take over their living spaces and the food they eat. Other invasive species that have been moved around by people include rats, dogs, rabbits, various plants, and even crayfish (which are like lobsters).

Fast Facts

Name: Common starling
Size: 20 cm (8 in) long
Home: Towns and suburbs almost worldwide
Eats: Insects, worms, other small animals

SOME MAMMALS LAY EGGS

One of the things that defines a mammal is that it gives birth to live young rather than laying eggs. Cats, dogs, people, lions, mice ... they don't hatch from eggs. But there are a few mammals that do. They're called monotremes, and there are only two types—platypuses and echidnas. They live in Australia and the nearby regions of New Guinea and New Zealand.

A LITTLE BIT REPTILE

Mammals evolved from reptiles, which lay eggs that have either a hard shell or a tough, leathery outside. Reptiles are cold-blooded (they don't produce their own body heat) and they have scales. Monotremes are warm-blooded (they produce body heat) and they have fur, like other mammals, but they lay eggs, like reptiles.

LICK IT UP

Like other mammals, monotremes produce milk to feed their babies. But unlike other mammals, the mother doesn't have teats the babies can suck milk from. Instead, the milk oozes directly from her skin in a special patch on her front. The babies have to lick it up.

Fast Facts

Name: Platypus
Size: Body 38 cm (15 in) long, plus tail 13 cm (5 in) long
Home: Rivers in eastern Australia
Eats: Insects, worms, shellfish

TRULY WEIRD

Monotremes are odd in lots of ways. Platypuses can sense electric currents produced by other animals (like electric eels can), which they use to find their food. Platypuses also have a leathery beak like a duck's bill—which is why they are called duck-billed platypuses. They look so bizarre that when European naturalists first saw a dead playpus, they thought it was a fake animal, put together from bits and pieces of others!

GIRAFFES CREEP UP ON TREES

Giraffes eat the leaves of trees. You wouldn't think that it's necessary to creep up on a tree, since it can't see you (or a giraffe) coming, and it can't run away. Even so, giraffes often approach a tree by coming from the opposite direction from the wind, so the wind is blowing toward the giraffe. Can trees smell a giraffe? Not quite ...

GIRAFFES VERSUS TREES

Giraffes like acacia trees and eat a lot of them—up to 29 kg (64 lb) of leaves and twigs each day. This is obviously bad news for the tree. So when they're bitten by a giraffe, the trees produce a substance called tannin. It's the chemical that gives tea its bitterness. Giraffes don't like tannin, so they stop eating and move to another tree. Tannin carried on the wind warns any trees downwind of the one being nibbled, and they start to produce their own tannin. Giraffes outwit the trees by moving on to a tree upwind of the one they've nibbled, taking the tree by surprise.

Fast Facts

Name: Giraffe
Size: 4.3–5.7 m
(14 ft 1 in–18 ft 8 in) tall
Home: African grasslands,
open woodlands
Eats: Leaves, twigs,
grass, fruit

ARMS RACE

Giraffes versus acacia trees is just one example of organisms struggling to outwit each other. The one that's being eaten develops new ways of defending itself or avoiding becoming lunch, and the one doing the eating works to find ways around the protective measures.

Buzz off and find your own dinner!

Some can be quite inventive or sneaky. When maize is eaten by a caterpillar it produces chemicals that attract a type of wasp. The wasps are parasitic—they lay their eggs in the caterpillars, eventually killing them. Perhaps acacia trees need to start producing a chemical that attracts lions!

SOME SHARKS ARE REALLY, REALLY OLD

The Greenland shark lives mostly in the Arctic waters around Greenland. It's thought to be the longest-lived vertebrate (animal with a backbone) and can reach the very old age of 400 to 500 years.

COLD AND SLOW

In general, big animals tend to live longer than small ones. Although a Greenland shark is big, at 7 m (23 ft) long, it's not as big as a blue whale—yet it lives five times as long as the whale. Why? The shark has a very low metabolic rate, meaning that it uses little energy and lives entirely in slow motion. It takes 150 years to grow old enough to reproduce and swims at only 1.2 km/h (0.75 mph). It's so slow and dopey that one of its names is sleeper shark.

DISCOVER A SHARK'S AGE

Scientists can't ask a shark how old it is or count the candles on its birthday cake. Instead, they need to find out its age from its body. Many sharks have growth rings on their vertebrae (sections of their backbone), and these can be counted like tree rings to work out how old the shark is.

Fast Facts

Name: Greenland shark
Size: 2.4–7 m (7 ft 11 in–23 ft)
Home: North Atlantic Ocean
Eats: Fish, seals

Greenland sharks don't have rings on their vertebrae, though. But the shark does keep adding layers to the lens inside its eye during its lifetime. By taking material from the middle of the lens, scientists can work out the approximate age of the shark using carbon dating (a way of working out the age of something from the carbon it contains). It's not as accurate as counting rings, and you can't do it until the shark is dead.

VULTURES WET THEMSELVES

And not just because they forget to pee before they fly out on a trip—they do it on purpose. Turkey vultures often live in hot places, and they pee down their legs as a way of cooling themselves down. As the water evaporates, it draws heat away from their bodies. The birds can't sweat to lose heat, so this is the best option.

TAKING THE HEAT OFF

Animals have many different ways of cooling down when they're too hot. Reptiles can't control their own body temperature, so they hide in a shady place where the surroundings are cooler, or even burrow underground. But mammals and birds produce heat within their bodies, so if the surroundings are also hot, they can overheat.

I can't go when you're watching!

If you get too hot, you start to sweat. Water oozes out onto the surface of your skin, where it is warmed by the blood beneath. As it evaporates, heat is lost to the air. A dog pants for the same reason. Water evaporates from its tongue more easily than it could evaporate from a fur-covered body. Some birds use a similar trick. They flutter their beak open and shut, moving air over the inside of the mouth to help water evaporate.

Everyone knows that squirrels are cool.

FLAT OUT

Some animals lose heat by spreading out so that they have a larger body surface area. Air moving over their body whisks away some of the heat. Ground squirrels flatten themselves on the ground so that some of their body heat is lost to the cooler earth below them.

SOME BIRDS START FIRES

Indigenous people in Australia have known for thousands of years that firehawks start wildfires. It might sound like a myth to explain the fires that ravage the country, but it's true. Some birds of prey, including black kites, whistling kites, and brown falcons, carry burning sticks and drop them to start a new fire.

Who ordered the barbecue?

FIRE FROM ABOVE

Fires start in many ways in the hot, dry Australian outback, including lightning and people having campfires that get out of hand. Birds are another, unexpected cause. Some scientists resist the idea that firehawks start the fires on purpose, but it seems reasonable. The birds eat small animals, birds, and insects. When a firehawk drops a flaming stick onto dry grass, it starts a fire that leads to all of these tasty snacks rushing from the area. The firehawk can then swoop in for the kill.

HOT AND COLD TOOLS

Humans aren't the only animals to use tools. It's well known that other primates (monkeys and apes) use them, too. They use stones to crack nuts, long sticks to scoop ants from their nests, strong sticks to dig up roots, and even sharpened twigs to spear small animals sleeping in trees. Dolphins, meanwhile, cover their sensitive noses with a sponge while foraging over rough rocks. And some crows make hooks from plants to extract insects from holes. Even so, deliberately starting a fire takes cunning up a level!

Fast Facts

Name: Black kite
Size: Wingspan 1.5 m (4 ft 11 in)
Home: Europe, Asia, Africa, and Australia
Eats: Small mammals, carrion, fish, birds

POLAR BEARS ARE BLACK

You may know that polar bears have white fur, but did you know that their skin is black? If you ever get the chance to look under their feet, you'll see that the pads are black. And their black noses are easy to spot.

PINK AND BLACK

Polar bear cubs are born pink with a coating of white fuzz. Even their foot pads and nose are pink at this stage. Then, when they're three or four months old, their skin starts to turn black. And not just the outside of the polar bear—even the lips, tongue, and inside the mouth become at least speckled with black and sometimes entirely black.

Fast Facts

Name: Polar bear
Size: Males 2–2.5 m
 (6 ft 7 in–8 ft 2 in) long,
 females 1.8–2 m
 (5 ft 11 in–6 ft 7 in) long
Home: Arctic
Eats: Seals, small whales,
 reindeer, birds

HOT AND COLD, BLACK AND WHITE

No one is entirely sure why polar bears go black, but it's likely to be to do with managing the heat and ultraviolet (UV) radiation from sunlight. UV radiation is damaging to most animals. It's what causes you to become sunburned if you spend too long in the sun without protection. White surfaces reflect UV and other radiation in sunlight. Since polar bears spend a lot of time around white snow and highly reflective ice, they're bombarded by UV from all around. Their white fur helps to reflect it away from them.

But they then have a black layer which does the opposite. It absorbs heat from sunlight, keeping the bear a bit warmer. Dark skin, in both bears and people, helps to protect from sunburn, too. The pigment that makes skin dark is called melanin and it prevents damage by UV light.

Could you rub some on my back for me?

41

A FLEA CAN JUMP 50 TIMES ITS BODY LENGTH

You can't do that. If you were, let's say, 1.2 m (4 ft) tall, you'd have to jump 60 m (200 ft) to match the flea's mighty leap. Your muscles don't work in a way that could lift your body weight that far. A flea, though, doesn't only have muscles—it has a special elastic springy mechanism that stores energy and hurls the flea into the air.

BOING!

Fleas have a pad of an elastic protein above their back legs and spines near their back feet, which grip the ground before they jump. As they bend their legs, the elastic pad is compressed (squashed). When they release their muscles to jump, the elastic boings back into shape and the legs act like multijointed levers pushing against the ground. The laws of physics mean that an equal force pushes the flea upward, hurling it into the air.

Fast Facts

Name: Human flea
Size: Up to 4 mm (0.15 in)
Home: Worldwide, on a human host
Eats: Blood

STRETCHY MUSCLES

When the muscles in your arms or legs are relaxed (not working), they're long. When they work, they contract. This pulls on a bone to which they're attached. It's a simple mechanical system. When you want to jump, you bend your knees, which you do by contracting (shortening) muscles to bring your lower leg closer to your upper leg. Your knee works like a hinge.

When you jump, you push against the ground—just like a flea does—but instead of an elastic spring to bounce you into the air, you rely on muscles releasing energy to suddenly straighten your leg and force you upward off the ground. Although they're good for jumping, they're no match for a built-in spring.

SOME BIRDS HAVE CLAWS ON THEIR WINGS

The hoatzin is a type of bird that lives in the Amazonian rain forests of South America. Hoatzin chicks have claws on their wings—not on the ends of the feathers, but coming out of the bend of the wing. You might think of the bend as being like an elbow, but it's really the chick's wrist, and the claws are on tiny fingers. They can use their claws to grip the tree and clamber around through the branches without falling.

CLAWS FOR CLIMBING

Birds can't fly as soon as they hatch. Although some hatch with fuzzy feathers, they don't have flight feathers and have to wait in the nest until these grow in. Baby hoatzins sometimes jump out of their nest trees if they're in danger of attack by a predator. They drop into the river below, swim underwater to their nest tree, and then clamber out. Without flight feathers, they could get stuck on the ground. But because hoatzins can hook their strong claws into the bark, they can haul themselves upward to climb back to the nest.

Fast Facts

Name: Hoatzin
Size: 65 cm (26 in) long
Home: Mangroves of northern
South America
Eats: Leaves

I'm looking for my great-great-great-great-great-great-great-great-great-great-great-great-great-great-great-granddaughter.

CLAWED ANCESTORS

Modern birds have evolved from ancestors descended from dinosaurs with front limbs like those of other land-going animals. These had one upper and two lower arm bones, then a wrist with fingers. Many dinosaurs had large claws on these fingers. When birds evolved from them, they at first kept three fingers with claws that stuck out through the feathers. Most birds have now lost these entirely, but hoatzin chicks still have two claws. They lose them only once they become fully feathered.

SHARKS "SEE" WITH ELECTRICITY

All animals generate tiny electric currents in their bodies as they move their muscles. Sharks have special cells in their heads that can pick up the electricity produced by other animals. They use this information to find those animals, and then they eat them.

NERVOUS ENERGY

All animals have nerves. They connect muscles to the central nervous system, which in humans is the spinal cord and the brain. The brain sends signals to the muscles, and receives information from sensory receptors, such as eyes and ears, in the form of tiny electric charges passing along the nerves.

Fast Facts

Name: Great white shark
Size: 4–5 m (13 ft 2 in–16 ft 5 in) long
Home: Warm oceans around the world
Eats: Fish, sea mammals (including whales and dolphins), seabirds

EXTRA SENSE

You can tell what's around you by using your senses to see, hear, smell, taste, and touch objects. Some animals have an extra sense—sharks and some other fish pick up the slight electric fields produced by other animals and then home in on them to gobble them up. Electricity is produced by muscle movements, so an animal moving vigorously produces more electricity. This is rather a nuisance. It means that if you fall off a boat in an ocean where sharks live, then thrashing around to stay afloat or attract someone's attention will also attract nearby sharks.

BEE ELECTRIC

It's not only fish that use electricity. Bees also detect electric fields, and can even pick up the electricity of plants. Some flowers have a different electric field after they've been visited by a bee, so then other bees don't bother to visit them.

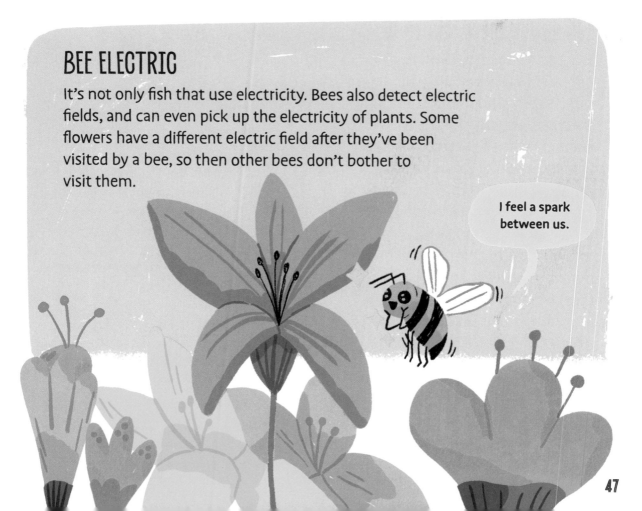

I feel a spark between us.

EVERY NINE-BANDED ARMADILLO IS ONE OF QUADRUPLETS

Do you have a twin—a brother or sister born at the same time as you? It's not uncommon. It's much less common for three or four babies to be born at once. But nine-banded armadillos almost always have four identical babies at once. No one knows why.

THE SAME OR DIFFERENT?

Twins can either be identical or non-identical. Identical twins are the same sex (male or female) and look the same. They're genetically identical—they have the same DNA (genetic material). Non-identical twins can be different sexes, and can look similar or different, just as other brothers and sisters can. Lots of types of animals have multiple babies at once, but they're not identical. A cat or dog, for example, has a mix of male and female babies at the same time.

Fast Facts

Name: Nine-banded armadillo
Size: Body 38–58 cm (15–23 in) long, plus tail 26–53 cm (10–21 in) long
Home: North, Central, and South America
Eats: Insects, mostly termites

ONE OR TWO EGGS

For a baby to be created, an egg cell must first be fertilized by a sperm cell. It then divides, making new cells. Over time, the cells produce all the organs and tissues of the body, creating a baby. It's the same in all animals, including armadillos.

How come I got the name Spot?

Occasionally, in humans, two egg cells can be fertilized and begin to grow, becoming non-identical twins. And sometimes a single fertilized egg splits into two and both halves develop into a baby. These become identical twins. In a nine-banded armadillo, it seems that the egg cell always splits in two, and the two new cells also split, giving four. Then each of the four cells begins to grow into identical armadillo quadruplets.

A BEE CAN TELL IF YOU HAVE COVID-19

Medical doctors have several ways of telling whether someone is ill, but one of the most unusual is using animals to sniff it out! Bees can be trained to spot people with COVID-19, rats can identify people with TB (tuberculosis), and dogs can spot a host of conditions and even tell when someone with epilepsy is about to have a seizure.

I prescribe a teaspoon of honey every day.

Fast Facts

Name: Western honey bee
Size: 1–1.5 cm (0.4–0.6 in) long
Home: Worldwide
Eats: Pollen, nectar

TRAINED ANTS?

Even ants can be trained to spot mice with cancer. Ants are cheap and easy to keep, and it takes only three training sessions lasting just 10 minutes each before they can correctly identify mice with cancer.

Scientists hope to use them with human patients. A urine sample shown to ants would be a quick and easy first step in diagnosis, moving the person toward the treatment they need. The ants are trained by giving them a sugary reward when they correctly identify urine that smells of cancer.

Scientists don't know exactly which chemicals animals are smelling when they pick up hints of disease. Smell training is useful outside of medicine, too. Rats have been trained to find landmines by smell, and by 2023, they had helped people clear 150,000 mines.

Fetch!

HOW TO TRAIN YOUR ANT

Training an ant or other animal in this way is called operant conditioning. The ant is taught to associate a sugary reward with the smell scientists want it to find. Very soon, the ant will move toward samples with the right smell even if there's not immediately any sugar beside it. So long as they're consistently rewarded, they'll keep moving toward the smell.

FLAMINGOS DON'T START OUT PINK

Flamingo chicks have white or ashy fluffy feathers when they hatch. They only turn pink when they've eaten enough of the food that gives their feathers pink pigment. If flamingos are kept in captivity, they have to be fed the right food to keep them pink or else their feathers go dull.

PINK, BUT TOUGH

Flamingos stand in water that's so alkaline (the opposite of acidic) that it could burn the flesh from your bones—but flamingos are just fine with it. This water contains algae, crustaceans (such as shrimp) that eat the algae, and flamingos that eat both. The algae produce a chemical called carotene (which is also found in carrots). A flamingo's body breaks this down into pigments called carotenoids. These build up in its feathers—and also in its fat, skin, and the yolks of its eggs, all of which are stained pink or orange.

Deep pink is *so* this season!

PINK, RED, ORANGE

The exact shade of a flamingo's feathers depends on its diet. Flamingos like their partners to be *really* pink. The brightest birds can most easily attract a mate. This is probably because the deeper pink they are, the more food they have found—and being very good at finding food is desirable in a mate.

DRINK YOUR MILK!

Flamingo parents produce something called crop milk from their throat, which they use to feed their chicks. This is also bright pink, because the parent bird concentrates pigment in it to get the baby off to a good, pink start.

Fast Facts

Name: Greater flamingo
Size: 1.1 m–1.5 m
(3 ft 7 in–4 ft 11 in) tall
Home: Mudflats and shallow lagoons in parts of Africa, southern Europe, south and southwest Asia
Eats: Shrimp, blue-green algae

RHINOS WERE ONCE AS TALL AS A HOUSE

Paraceratherium was a large ancestor of modern rhinos. It lived in Tibet about 30 million years ago and was the largest mammal that has ever lived on land. The biggest type weighed as much as six elephants. Its shoulders were nearly 5 m (16 ft 5 in) from the ground, and its head was 7 m (23 ft) from the ground—a good deal higher than a giraffe's. It was 8 m (26 ft) long, too.

Fast Facts

Name: *Paraceratherium*
Size: 5 m (16 ft 5 in) to the shoulder
Home: Eurasia, 34–23 million years ago
Ate: Leaves

BIGGER AND BIGGER

Once an animal starts to get big, some factors make it carry on getting even bigger. *Paraceratherium* needed a lot of food, but leaves are hard to digest and don't provide much nourishment. The large animal needed to eat a lot, so it needed a large gut to process the leaves. Then it needed to be bigger to support a large gut, and then it needed even more food because it was larger ...

WHY SO BIG?

Paraceratherium was a browser, meaning that it ate leaves from trees. By growing large, *Paraceratherium* could reach leaves that other animals couldn't. This is important, since if all animals are trying to eat exactly the same type of food, the landscape can't support as many of them as it can if they eat different foods. Being very large, it had to feed almost all the time and so it needed a lot of leaves. It had to roam over a large area to get enough food. Long, sturdy legs meant that it could take large strides and cover a lot of ground in its hunt for food.

ANTS MAKE GREAT FARMERS

But rather small farmers. They don't farm cattle, pigs, or maize as people do. They farm fungus and aphids (greenfly). But they do it in similar ways, raising and looking after their crops or livestock.

LEAFCUTTER ANTS DON'T EAT LEAVES

If you've ever seen leafcutter ants, in real life or on a screen, you'll know that they snip out part of a leaf and then carry it away. But they don't then eat the leaves. Instead, they use the leaves in their fungus farm, deep inside their ant nest. The fungus grows on the leaves as they rot, and the ants feed on the fungus, though not all of it.

Both the ants and the fungus benefit, in a relationship called mutualism. The fungus doesn't need to produce spores to reproduce since the ants spread it around the forest and then bring food to it. In return, the ants eat a small part of the fungus. You could say that the fungus is farming the ants!

MILKING APHIDS

When there are greenfly on a plant, there are often ants nearby. The ants look after the aphids, keeping away other insects that would like to eat them. The ants don't eat the aphids themselves. Instead, they milk them, sipping sweet liquid called honeydew which the aphids make. To get the aphids to ooze out honeydew, the ants stroke them on the abdomen. The aphids even let the ants move them around on and between plants. The arrangement benefits both of them—the ants get food, and the aphids avoid being eaten.

You're so sweet!

SLOTHS CAN BE GREEN

Sloths live in the trees of the South American rain forest. Like all mammals, they have hair. No mammals have green fur—yet sloths are green. Their fur isn't green itself, but the sloth moves so slowly that algae grow on it, making it appear green.

PERFECT DISGUISE

You might get annoyed if algae grew on your hair, and you'd probably want to wash it off. But for a sloth, it's very useful. Sloths make a welcome snack for harpy eagles, which snatch them from the treetops, or jaguars and ocelots, which take them lower down. Moving slowly means that they don't attract the attention of predators on the lookout for a meal. And being green keeps them hidden among the leaves! In return, the algae get a nice place to live, as well as water, because sloth fur tends to stay soggy.

I like to blend in.

Fast Facts

Name: Three-toed sloth
Size: 45 cm (18 in) long
Home: Forests of northern
and central South America
Eats: Leaves

SLOWLY DOES IT

Sloths live their whole lives in slow motion. They sleep for between 15 and 20 hours a day, creep slowly through the trees, and come to the forest floor to poop only once a week. It takes a long time to digest their food—days or even weeks. They keep their stomach topped up with a few leaves each day in the moments when they're awake.

SLOTHWORLD

Because it stays still so much of the time, a sloth is home to a whole community of living things. There's even a type of moth that lives on its fur and lays eggs in its poop. When the eggs hatch, the larvae feed on the sloth-droppings. When they mature, they fly onto a sloth to make their home.

THERE ARE PENGUINS IN THE FORESTS OF NEW ZEALAND

We think of penguins as living in icy Antarctica. But on the Snare Islands, New Zealand, 60,000 penguins live in the forest, and often enjoy quite warm weather. They even sometimes perch in trees!

I thought YOU had the map!

FAMILIAR LIFESTYLE

Aside from living somewhere warmer, and with trees, Snares penguins have lives similar to their cousins' in colder places. They make long foraging trips to the sea, where they catch krill, squid, and fish to eat. Parents take it in turns to look after the eggs. They nest together in large colonies.

But unlike penguins that nest on windblown ice, the forest penguins make a nest on the ground by forming a hollow in the soil and building a mud rim around it. They line it with grass and twigs. The colonies are so large that the nesting destroys vegetation in the area, and they have to move on to another site next time. Penguins in the Antarctic, by contrast, keep the eggs on their feet, protected from the ice beneath and warmed by the parent's body.

A CUSHY LIFE?

When a group of animals is isolated in one place, as Snares penguins are, they often evolve into a new species. After thousands or millions of years, their bodies and how they behave change to suit their new conditions. That's how penguins originally got their layer of fat to keep them warm, and their streamlined shape for swimming. Snares penguins don't look very different from other penguins, but how they act has changed to suit a life in the forest.

Fast Facts

Name: Snares penguin
Size: 50–70 cm (20–28 in) tall
Home: Forests of Snares Islands, New Zealand
Eats: Krill, fish, cephalopods (such as squid and octopuses)

New Zealand sounds nice but Antarctica is cooler.

THERE'S A JELLYFISH THAT FLASHES LIKE A POLICE CAR

The Atolla jellyfish flashes thousands of blue lights that are visible to prey and predators in the dark of the deep ocean. It seems to flash its lights in a circle running around its body as an alarm call when it's in danger. The lights attract larger predators that could eat whatever was threatening Atolla. This unusual trick has earned it the nickname alarm jellyfish.

DEEP AND RED

The jellyfish itself is deep red, but red light doesn't reach the depths where it lives, so it looks black to its prey and predators. A black jellyfish in a black sea isn't visible. The flashing lights then come as a surprise to predators that think they are just circling in the darkness.

NO BATTERIES

The Atolla jellyfish is one of many deep-sea creatures that make their own light. Anglerfish have an illuminated lure hanging in front of their mouths. Inquisitive fish that swim toward the light are quickly gobbled up. In some places, vast swarms of glowing plankton in the sea make the sea itself glow at certain times.

I was hoping for more than a light bite.

All these glowing organisms are bioluminescent—they make light using chemicals. A chemical reaction takes place in their bodies which produces energy. Unlike most reactions, which produce energy as heat, this reaction releases energy as light. Some bioluminescent animals don't make the light themselves—they either eat bacteria or plankton that glow, or keep these glowing helpers inside them.

HORNED LIZARDS SPIT BLOOD— FROM THEIR EYES

If a predator creeps up on a short-horned lizard, it's in for a surprise. The lizard spurts a jet of blood up to 1.5 m (4 ft 11 in) at its attacker. A stream of blood pouring from the eyes of your intended meal would probably put you off your food, and it does for most lizard predators, too.

Don't call me a squirt!

BLOW UP YOUR EYES?

The lizard has muscles near its eyes which can cut off the blood flow from the eye back to the heart, but blood still flows to the eye. As more blood comes in, pressure builds up, until eventually a blood vessel bursts and blood shoots out. To make it even worse, the blood tastes horrible and is possibly toxic.

Fast Facts

Name: Texas horned lizard
Size: 7–11.4 cm (3–4.5 in) long
Home: Grasslands and shrublands in Mexico and the USA
Eats: Ants, other insects

OTHER NIFTY TRICKS

Horned lizards aren't the only animals to pull cool tricks to drive away predators. Some animals try to look bigger than they really are. A pufferfish, for example, inflates itself like a balloon, making spikes stand up all over its body. The idea of swallowing a spiky ball drives away most hungry fish.

If you have a pet cat, you might have seen it arch its back and fluff up its fur. That's the same trick as the one used by the pufferfish, but toned down a bit. The cat's trying to look big and scary. Some lizards will break their tail off to distract a predator. The tail keeps on wriggling while the lizard runs away. In time, the lizard grows a new tail, so it can repeat the trick if necessary!

SOME ANIMALS KEEP THEIR BABIES IN A POCKET

Lots of animals carry their babies around with them, on their backs or their fronts. But marsupial mothers have a pouch on the front of their bodies which is just for that purpose. Marsupials include koalas, kangaroos, wallabies, opossums, and wombats. Most live in Australasia.

MILK ON DEMAND

Marsupial babies are born tiny, blind, furless, and with their bodies only partly developed. They crawl straight to the mother's pouch where they hide inside and grow. The mother has one or more teats in her pouch which produce milk. The baby attaches itself to the teat and stays there, feeding and growing. When it's big enough, it pokes its head out of the pouch. By this time, it's fully formed and has fur, and its eyes are open. After a few weeks, it begins to venture out from the pouch, but still scrambles back inside for safety and a drink of milk.

Fast Facts

Name: Red kangaroo
Size: Body up to 1.6 m (5 ft 3 in) long, plus tail 1.2 m (3 ft 11 in) long
Home: Grassland, scrubland, and desert in Australia
Eats: Grass, other plants

UNDERDEVELOPED BABIES

Baby animals vary hugely in how dependent on their parents they are. A panda baby is only 15 cm (6 in) long—just one hundredth the length of an adult panda. That's as if you were just 1.8 cm (0.7 in) long when you were a baby! Pandas don't have a pouch and have to be careful they don't accidentally squash their tiny babies.

At the other extreme, baby deer can stand and run soon after birth. They need to, since lots of predators are on the lookout for an easy meal. Most baby mammals fall somewhere between the super-vulnerable panda-style baby and the independent baby deer.

A STARFISH THROWS UP ITS STOMACH TO EAT

When you eat, you put food in your mouth and swallow it to get it down into your stomach. Your stomach stays in the same place and waits for the food to arrive. But a starfish does it the other way around. It finds a tasty meal and sends its stomach out to get it.

INSIDE IS OUTSIDE

When it finds a yummy-looking clam or other shellfish, a starfish turns its stomach inside out and then pops it out of its mouth. The stomach digests what it can of the meal (leaving the shell), turning it into a kind of sludgy chowder. Then the starfish sucks its stomach back inside with the meal inside it.

I'll show you that I have guts!

POOP ON YOUR HEAD?

Starfish have two parts to their stomach. The second part (not the bit that gets vomited out and sucked in) has extensions that go into each of the starfish's arms. That means that food goes in the bottom side, is digested in the middle and in the arms, and then the waste comes out through a hole on the top. Yes, a starfish's butt is on top of it. This means that unless the current washes it away, the poop stays on top of its head. Or where its head would be if it had one. Since it has no central brain to put in it, no nose, no ears, and its eyes are on each arm, it has no need of a head.

Fast Facts

Name: Bloody Henry starfish
Size: 10 cm (4 in) across
Home: Sea around the UK
Eats: Small animals in the sea; also filters smaller particles from the water

SOME FISH CAN WALK

Frogfish "walk" over the seabed using their pectoral fins. This kind of fish lies in wait for prey rather than swimming after it. Creeping about on the ground might help make it look unfishlike. It shuffles along, relying on the water to hold it up so that it bounces from one fin to the other.

MISTAKEN IDENTITY

The fish was named "frogfish" in 1734 when people believed that it was an amphibian and could use its legs on land. A study in 2012 found that if you put the fish on dry land it just lies down, spread out like a pancake, and can't walk at all.

FISH ON LAND

Frogfish aren't the only ones that walk. Lungfish use their back fins to push themselves up and along. Lungfish, as their name suggests, have lungs and can also breathe air, which helps them survive if the pools they live in dry out. Lungfish are probably related to the first four-legged animals to walk on Earth.

Around 380 million years ago, fish with strong, proplike fins dragged themselves up riverbanks or beaches onto land. They were a type of lobe-finned fish, which means that they had a thick, fleshy lobe above the frilly part of their fins. This could contain muscles (which a normal frilly fin can't) and so could work like a leg.

The first amphibians evolved from them, and other land-going animals evolved from amphibians—reptiles, birds, and mammals. That's why all these have a similar body plan of a head, neck, four limbs, and often a tail.

SPIDERS HAVE BLUE BLOOD

You have red blood, but not everything does! Spiders and horseshoe crabs both have pale blue blood. Some octopuses and scorpions have blue blood, too. Some caterpillars, leeches, and skinks (a type of lizard) have green blood. Beetles have yellow blood, and cockroaches have white blood, while a strange cold-water fish called an icefish has completely see-through blood.

It only hurts when I laugh.

Fast Facts

Name: Tarantula (there are many other types of spiders)
Size: Up to 11 cm (4.3 in) across the body, up 30 cm (12 in) across the legs
Home: Across the southern hemisphere (different types), USA, and parts of Europe and Asia
Eats: Large insects, other arthropods

DELIVERING OXYGEN

Blood travels around the body of an animal delivering oxygen to different parts. The animal's tissues and organs need oxygen to function. The oxygen is carried in the blood by chemicals called proteins. All vertebrates (animals with a backbone) use a protein called hemoglobin to carry oxygen, but other animals use different proteins.

Some of these proteins make blood blue, others make it green, yellow, or white. The icefish lives in very cold water. Since cold water can carry much more oxygen than warmer water, the fish doesn't need any proteins to carry the oxygen in its blood—there's enough there already—so its blood can be clear.

I should have worn my mittens today.

BLOODLESS

Vertebrates have complicated bodies, with lungs that take air into the body and a heart that pumps blood around it. Oxygen in the air passes into the blood in the lungs. Insects are small and have no lungs. Instead, they have holes called spiracles in the sides of their bodies. Oxygen from the air is taken in through these holes. And some animals are so simple that they don't even have blood. These include jellyfish, sponges, and corals.

ANTEATERS WALK ON THEIR KNUCKLES

You walk flat on your feet, and four-footed animals such as cats and dogs also put their paws flat on the ground. But anteaters and a few other animals walk with their back feet flat on the floor, while their front feet curl around so that their knuckles rest on the ground. You'd probably find it very uncomfortable to do that, but they're specially adapted to do it.

I hate to chip my fingernails!

CURLED CLAWS

Anteaters and sloths have very long claws. Sloths use them to grip onto tree bark as they climb through trees. Anteaters use their long claws to rip through ant nests to find the insects they eat. To protect their claws, sloths and anteaters fold their "fingers" back as they walk on the ground. Their claws could easily trip them up or get broken if they didn't do this.

Fast Facts

Name: Chimpanzee
Size: 1.5 m (4 ft 11 in) tall
Home: Grasslands and
  forests of Africa
Eats: Insects, honey, small
  mammals, nuts, fruit

CLOSER TO US

Like us, gorillas and chimpanzees are primates, and they sometimes walk on their knuckles. These animals have long fingers, like ours. If they walked on all fours with the fingers splayed, the fingers would easily get caught. Folding them out of the way keeps them safe.

I don't see the resemblance.

GIANT KNUCKLE-DRAGGERS

Long ago, some very large animals walked on their knuckles. *Megatherium* was a giant ground sloth that lived from 5 million years ago until about 10,000 years ago. It grew to 6 m (19 ft 8 in) long. *Chalicotherium* lived 15–5 million years ago. It was a bizarre animal with a snout like a horse and the body of a moose. It was about 2.7 m (8 ft 10 in) tall to the shoulder and walked on its knuckles.

PUFFINS GLOW IN ULTRAVIOLET LIGHT

We can see only in visible light, which is the part of the electromagnetic spectrum that runs from red to violet light. But there are other types of electromagnetic radiation outside of the narrow range that we can see. Ultraviolet is just beyond violet. A bulb that glows ultraviolet doesn't seem to us to glow at all, but some animals can see it. And some things, including puffins, glow when ultraviolet falls on them. No one knows how this helps the birds.

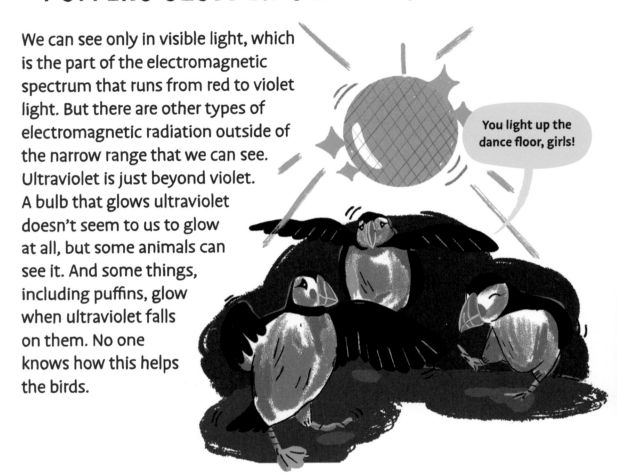

You light up the dance floor, girls!

BRIGHT BEAKS

A puffin is a chubby black-and-white bird with a large brightly striped beak. It lives near the coast in northern seas and dives for fish. Just its beak glows under an ultraviolet lamp, not the whole puffin. Their glowiness was first discovered when a researcher shone an ultraviolet lamp on a puffin preserved in a museum. It would show up nicely in disco lighting, though puffins don't usually go to discos!

BEYOND LIGHT

Some animals can see in ultraviolet. They have access to a whole world that is hidden to us. Many flowers have patterns that show up only in ultraviolet, showing the direction an insect must follow to reach the flower's pollen. Insects that can see in ultraviolet can then reach the pollen. They go on to carry it between different flowers, pollinating the plants. Bees and birds can see in ultraviolet. Whereas we see a dandelion as having plain yellow petals, bees see a change near the middle, guiding them to where they can collect pollen.

I'm coming in to land!

MILK COMES FROM WHALES. AND MICE. AND TIGERS ...

The milk you buy in a store usually comes from cows. Sometimes you might have goat milk, or even sheep or buffalo milk, but most milk is cow milk. Human babies often drink breast milk produced by their mothers. Cow, goat, sheep, and buffalo milk is produced by these animals for their babies. All mammals produce milk for their babies, including mice, tigers, whales, porcupines, polar bears, sloths, and bats.

BAT MILK? PORCUPINE CHEESE?

One of the defining features of a mammal is that the mother produces milk for her babies. Even mammals that live underwater, such as whales and dolphins, produce milk. The baby puts its mouth around the mother's teat, making a watertight seal, and can suck the milk without it leaking away into the sea. Humans don't generally use milk from wild animals, but in theory we could make cheese from porcupine milk, and take milk from bats—though it would take a lot of bats to get a useful amount.

Time to go vegan!

Fast Facts

Name: Common bottlenose dolphin
Size: 2.5–3.5 m (8 ft 2 in–11 ft 6 in) long
Home: Warm seas around the world
Eats: Fish, shrimp, cephalopods

THE PERFECT FOOD

Baby mammals require nourishment that's rich in the chemicals they need to grow. Many are born without teeth, and a lot can't move around on their own. A mother's milk takes nutrients from food she eats and concentrates them into milk that the baby can take without teeth, so there is no need to forage or hunt, or even to move around. As the baby animal grows bigger, it takes less milk and starts to eat the kind of food a grown-up animal eats.

SOME OWLS LIVE UNDERGROUND

Most owls live in holes in trees or sometimes in old buildings, but burrowing owls make their nests underground. They can make their burrows themselves or take over holes that have been made by other animals, including prairie dogs, tortoises, and armadillos. They're not the only birds that live in burrows—puffins do, too.

HOME FROM HOME IN A HOLE

The owls can make a burrow that is up to 3 m (9 ft 10 in) long, with a sleeping chamber at the end. It's not much of a nest, just a hole—they don't line it with anything snuggly. Some do line the tunnel to the nest with cow dung, though, which doesn't sound wonderful. But the dung probably attracts beetles and flies that the owls eat, providing in-house breakfast.

Fast Facts

Name: Burrowing owl
Size: 19–28 cm (7–11 in) long
Home: Grassland, desert, and other open ground of North and South America
Eats: Large insects, small mammals

In North America, the owls have traditionally lived in prairies, open grassland, and areas of bare soil. As people have driven away ground squirrels, armadillos, and prairie dogs, a shortage of holes has hit burrowing owls hard. Now, some owls are making their own holes in human areas with flat, open land and short grass—including airports and golf courses.

BEWARE OF PREDATORS

Most animals make their homes where they will be safe from predators, such as up a tree. So, are burrowing owls asking for trouble by living on the ground? Maybe, but they have a neat trick—they make a hissing noise like a rattlesnake, which frightens away animals that want to eat them!

Hssss!

A PLATYPUS HAS NO STOMACH

And it's not the only animal that's stomachless. Echidnas and about a quarter of all fish also have no stomach. Oddly, they all evolved from ancestors that did have a stomach and then they de-evolved them again!

Am I missing something?

WHO NEEDS A STOMACH ANYWAY?

The only animals that have stomachs are vertebrates (animals with a backbone). All the rest (invertebrates)—such as crabs, worms, spiders, slugs, jellyfish, sponges, and squids—have never had a stomach in the way we do.

Fast Facts

Name: Echidna
Size: Body 36–90 cm (14–35 in) long, plus tail 10 cm (4 in) long
Home: Australia, New Guinea
Eats: Ants, termites

UPSET STOMACH

Your stomach plays a big part in breaking down the food you eat. This is the first stage of digestion. It starts in your mouth, where your teeth chew food into small chunks and saliva (spit) begins to break it down chemically. Then you swallow the food. Its first stop is the stomach.

The stomach contains acidic liquid and enzymes (chemicals that speed up reactions), called pepsins. These begin to unpick the complex, large chemicals that make up proteins in food. Animals that eat food that's very tough to break down, such as coarse grasses, have more than one stomach, and food goes from one to another.

More cake will help me feel better ...

Essentially, a stomach is a large bag of acid and enzymes that start to break up chemicals in food before it passes into the intestine. The intestine is a long tube that partly digested food passes through, and enables useful chemicals from the food to be absorbed by the body. Many animals don't really need a stomach, so long as their bodies can still absorb nutrients from the food without the extra stage of chemical breakdown.

WE RELY ON BEETLES THAT EAT POOP

If you were a dung beetle, you'd be looking forward to tucking into a nice pile of animal droppings for your dinner. And for your breakfast and lunch. All they eat is stuff another animal has already eaten and then passed on out of its body. Yuck!

Yum! Fresh from the source!

POOP EVERYWHERE

Have you ever wondered why the world isn't covered in droppings? The answer is because they all get recycled. Dung beetles and other decomposers break down or eat them. This recycles the nutrients back into the soil, where they are taken up by growing plants, and the whole cycle can start over again. Without decomposers, the world couldn't function. Not only would we be neck-deep in poop, but the soil would run out of nutrients to feed plants, and there would be no plants for animals to eat.

FUSSY EATERS

You might think that you'd need to be pretty tolerant to live on a diet of poop, but dung beetles are quite fussy eaters. Different types of beetles eat different types of droppings. Give them the wrong food and they'll turn their noses up at it.

European settlers took cows to Australia, which naturally produced a lot of cowpats. Where cows have always lived, insects deal with the mess. But since there had not been cows previously in Australia, the right insects weren't available to do the job. So, the cowpats dried in a thick layer over huge areas of land. The grass couldn't grow through it and the land became useless. Eventually, dung beetles were brought in to clear up the mess.

Fast Facts

Name: Dung beetle (many types)
Size: Up to 3 cm (1.2 in)
Home: Everywhere except for Antarctica
Eats: Dung

DORMICE CAN SLEEP FOR 11 MONTHS

A dormouse is a very tiny mammal that weighs only 15–40 g (0.25–1.4 oz). Being so tiny, it loses heat quickly, so to survive the cold winter it goes into a sluggish state and hibernates. It also spends a lot of time asleep when it's not hibernating. Some opt for a super-long snooze if living conditions aren't great. A dormouse can live for five years, but it might be awake for only 5–15 months of that time.

HAVE A KID OR SLEEP?

Dormice eat a lot of seeds, especially the seeds of beech trees, called beech mast. Some years, the beech trees don't produce mast. When this happens, the dormice might go hungry. Any babies they had would struggle to survive. So, adults just eat what they can and go back to sleep again. They wait for the next year to see if conditions for raising babies improve.

Fast Facts

Name: Common dormouse
Size: Body 10 cm (4 in) long, plus tail 6 cm (2.4 in) long
Home: Northern Europe, west Asia
Eats: Berries, nuts (especially hazelnuts), insects, caterpillars

A GOOD SNOOZE

Many animals hibernate, sleeping through the winter. It's a way of saving energy when food is scarce. Mammals use energy from food to keep their body temperature stable. Running around outside in cold weather would use a lot of energy just keeping warm enough to survive. Instead, they curl up and sleep. They often hibernate underground, in a cave or hollow tree, or under piles of leaves or wood so that they're protected from the coldest weather. Their bodies slow down, they don't move, and they breathe more slowly. This means that they save energy and can live off the fat reserves they have built up over the summer.

Night, night! See you in spring!

THE HORNED SCREAMER IS A UNICORN-BIRD

Unicorns aren't real (sorry), but there are a few animals that have a horn growing from their heads. Some are familiar, such as the rhino and narwhal. But you've probably never seen a horned screamer. It's a bird about the size of a turkey and lives in South America. So far, so normal. But it has a long white horn growing from the front of its head, which is really not at all normal for birds. Indeed, it's the only bird that has anything like it.

Don't tell me unicorns don't exist!

HORNS, TUSKS, AND OTHER SPIKES

The horned screamer's horn is made of cartilage, which is a tough material that stiffens parts of bodies but isn't as hard as bone. You have cartilage in your nose and ears. It gives them shape, but can bend a bit without breaking, unlike bones. The screamer's horn can grow up to 15 cm (6 in) long. It sometimes gets broken off, but it can regrow. Other animals have horns made of different materials.

A rhino horn is made of keratin, which is the same material that makes up your fingernails and hair. A narwhal's horn is really a very long tusk, or adapted tooth. It's made of ivory (like elephant and walrus tusks), which is largely dentine—the material that makes the hard outside of teeth.

NO FIGHTING

Animals with horns often use them to defend themselves. Rhinos and narwhals use them to tussle over mates. Horned screamers' horns are too fragile to use as a weapon, though. No one knows what they are for, but they might make the birds attractive to mates.

TARDIGRADES COULD SURVIVE NUCLEAR WAR

Tardigrades—also named water bears or moss piglets—are tiny, eight-legged arthropods (jointed animals with a hard outside). Only about 1–2 mm (0.04–0.08 in) long, they live everywhere, from oceans to deserts, but they especially like damp moss or lichen. They really don't mind what the conditions are since they can survive extreme heat, cold, drought, and even radioactivity.

GOING TO EXTREMES

Tardigrades have been taken into space and are just fine when they come back. They're one of nature's survivors. After a zombie apocalypse or nuclear war, they'd just shrug and waddle off. Animals that can withstand extremely hostile conditions are called extremophiles. Tardigrades are winners even among extremophiles.

You'd have to try hard to annoy tardigrades. They can survive temperatures above the boiling point of water and as low as –270 °C (–454 °F). They can go without food and water for 30 years and still bounce back. They can put up with pressure six times that found at the bottom of the ocean, and tolerate the complete vacuum (no pressure) of space.

SHRINK TO SURVIVE

In a stressful situation, a tardigrade can squeeze all the water from its body, drying up completely, then roll into a ball and wait for conditions to improve. When they do, it rehydrates and goes about its usual business. A tardigrade can survive for years in its dehydrated form.

Fast Facts

Name: Tardigrade
Size: Up to 1.5 mm (0.06 in)
Home: Everywhere
Eats: Algae, plant cells, animal cells

STARTING OUT

The first life-forms on Earth might have been extremophile microbes. Today, extremophile microbes live deep within rock, in hot, acidic, volcanic pools, and far under the Antarctic ice.

LIMPETS HAVE MAGNETIC TEETH

Limpets are shellfish that spend their lives clinging to rocks. The limpet survives by eating algae off rocks by the shoreline. Like a snail, it has a radula—a set of many, very tiny teeth for scraping up food. But unlike a snail, its teeth are strengthened with an iron mineral and are magnetic. Limpet teeth are the hardest naturally occurring substance—five times stronger than spider silk, which was once thought to be the strongest.

MIGHTY MAGNETIC MOUTH

The limpet doesn't use the magnetic properties of its mouth—they just seem to be a side effect of its super-strong teeth. The teeth are made of very thin threads of an iron mineral (the magnetic part) strung through protein. The effect is rather like plastic reinforced with steel threads, but much stronger. It needs to be—the teeth have to be strong enough to scrape away rock without breaking.

ROCK-EATING HARD MAN

A limpet's radula is like a tongue bristling with hooked, daggerlike teeth. It would be really scary if it weren't so tiny (the teeth are less than 1 mm/0.04 in long). The limpet doesn't just scrape algae off the rocks, it also scrapes away the rock surface.

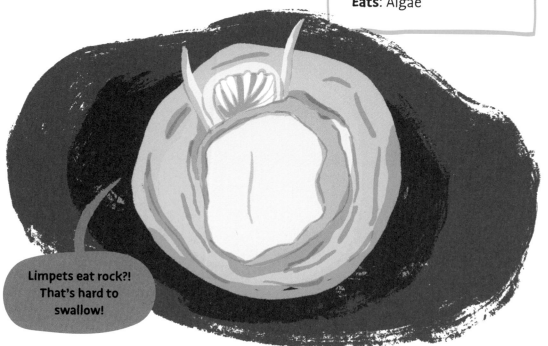

Limpets eat rock?! That's hard to swallow!

Inside the limpet, the algae is digested and the bits of rock come out the other end. Or, rather, the same end, since a limpet only has one end not covered by its shell. Its poop is also extra hard. Made of compressed and dried rock dust, limpet droppings are like concrete.

ANTS CAN BE EXPLOSIVE

As social insects, ants act as part of a colony rather than as individuals. But a type of ant in Borneo takes this to extremes, sacrificing itself to save its colony from predators by blowing itself up.

SECRET WEAPON

High in the treetops of the forests of Borneo lives an innocent-looking brown ant. It can't sting and doesn't have big, pinching jaws to bite hard. It doesn't look as though it would be much use at defending an ant colony. But if a predator threatens the ant and its comrades, the ant raises its back end in a warning gesture. If this doesn't work, the ant bites the attacker, directs its backside toward the predator, and tightens its muscles so much that its abdomen bursts open, showering poisonous yellow goo over the enemy. The goo kills larger ants and other insects, but it's also toxic to the exploding ant—as if blowing itself up wasn't enough to kill it!

Fast Facts

Name: *Colobopsis explodens*
Size: 8 mm (0.3 in) long
Home: Malaysia
Eats: Probably moss, lichen, algae

THE ULTIMATE SACRIFICE

The exploding ants aren't the only type to give up their lives to help their colony. A type of ant in Brazil seals up its nest each night so that predators can't find the ants and eat them. Most of the sealing is done from the inside, but a few ants stay outside to cover all traces of the entrance. They then can't get in, and most are dead by morning.

SOME OCTOPUSES ARM THEMSELVES WITH A DEAD JELLYFISH

Woo, scary! A jellyfish is a just a bag of goo! Actually, it *is* scary if you're a fish that might normally be killed by a jellyfish. The jellyfish is a big blob with tentacles hanging underneath. These tentacles can sting—that's how the jellyfish kills its prey. An octopus, which can't sting anything on its own, sometimes uses jellyfish tentacles as weapons.

DEADLY HUG

Some types of octopuses have been seen hugging dead jellyfish to them. After—or even while—sucking the innards out of the top of the jellyfish, they leave the long tentacles trailing. Although the jellyfish is dead, its poison lives on. A jellyfish can stay poisonous even weeks after it has died.

Fast Facts

Name: Seven-armed octopus
Size: Up to 3.9 m (12 ft 9 in)
Home: Atlantic Ocean
Eats: Jellyfish

HOW A JELLYFISH WORKS

Jellyfish tentacles are coated in lots of tiny stinging cells called cnidocytes (say "need-o-sites"). Each contains a tightly coiled thread filled with the jellyfish's poison. A trigger on the outside of the cell is activated if it touches something—such as a fish the jellyfish could eat, or an animal that might be attacking the jellyfish.

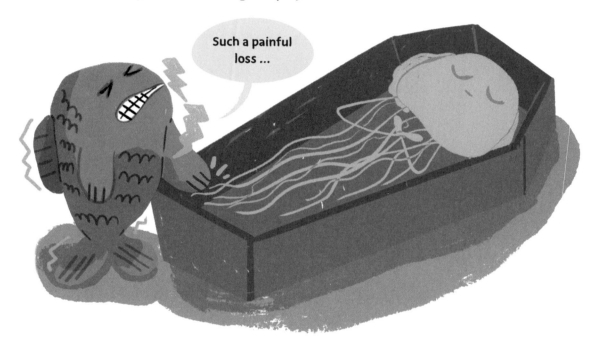

When the trigger is touched, the cell opens and the poisonous thread whizzes out. The sharp end pricks the victim, often breaking off and staying in its skin, causing pain and injury. It's entirely mechanical and doesn't rely on a brain (which is lucky, since jellyfish don't have one). This means that the tentacles still work after the jellyfish is dead, or if the tentacle has been ripped off and is carried by someone else—such as a crafty octopus.

SPIDER BABIES EAT THEIR MOTHER

The mother of one species of African spider makes the ultimate sacrifice—she lets her babies eat her. She first spits out nutritious liquid to feed her newly hatched babies, and then lets them dine on her. Even spider-aunts and friends are sometimes eaten. It might not sound like a good parenting strategy, but it ensures the youngsters survive to keep the family line going.

Now that's what I call a good parent!

PUTTING THE TIME IN

Other parents are self-sacrificing, too. The giant Pacific octopus spends up to four years guarding her eggs until they hatch. In that time, she doesn't eat. Not surprisingly, those babies are the death of her. But by guarding the eggs from predators, she makes sure the next generation survives to ... do the same.

EAT YOUR MATE!

It's not just mothers that come to a bad end. Females in several species of spider and insect eat the father after mating. And daddy anglerfish have to give up independent life. They attach themselves to the female and are locked there forever.

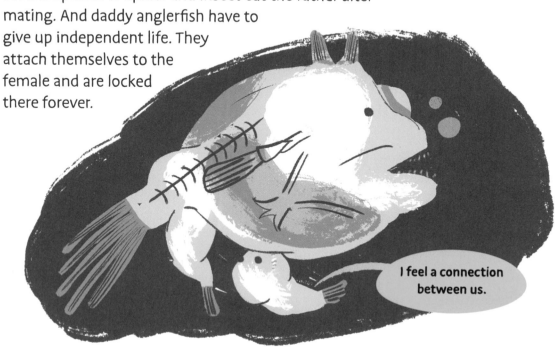

I feel a connection between us.

Fast Facts

Name: African social spider
Size: Up to 35 mm (0.14 in) long
Home: Central and southern Africa
Eats: Insects

INVEST IN THE FUTURE

In nature, animals and plants do what they can to reproduce, producing the next generation to keep their species going. They don't consciously aim to do it, but evolution benefits those that succeed in breeding and raising young, since their characteristics are passed on. Eating your mother might not sound like a desirable characteristic, but the spider-mother has served her purpose by having the babies. It's a hard world out there!

YOU CAN WORK OUT THE AGE OF A TORTOISE BY COUNTING ITS RINGS

Just as you can work out the age of a tree by counting the rings inside it—though only after cutting it down—you can work out the age of a tortoise by counting the rings on its shell. You don't need to look inside the tortoise, fortunately. The shell is made up of separate panels, called scutes, and these grow larger each year.

FROM TINY TO VAST

Tortoises start very small—often about the size of a coin—but even then they have all their scutes. As the tortoise grows, each scute becomes larger. Tortoises hibernate in the winter and only grow in the spring and summer. The season's growth makes a ring all around each scute, so by looking carefully at the scutes and counting their ridges, you can work out how old the tortoise is.

RINGS AND MORE RINGS

Tortoise scutes are far from the only animal part that lays down growth rings each year. The scales of many fish also build up year by year, and scientists can tell the age of the fish by counting the rings on the scales. Some shellfish, such as scallops, grow their shells from the middle, adding an extra ring each year. Most animals grow only, or mostly, in the spring and summer. Pauses between growing seasons mark the end of one ring and the start of the next.

My dad looks hard, but he's soft on the inside.

FaSt FaCtS

Name: Giant tortoise
Size: Up to 1.3 m (4 ft 3 in) long
Home: Islands of the Indian Ocean, Pacific Ocean, and the Caribbean, and the Galapagos Islands
Eats: Leaves

DID YOU KNOW?

The oldest known living tortoise was born around 1832. Called Jonathan, he lives on the island of St. Helena in the South Atlantic Ocean.

GIANT QUEEN ANTS CAN'T FEED THEMSELVES

A queen ant has one job—to lay eggs to produce the next generation. To do this, she grows enormously large. She is far larger than all the other ants in the ant colony, and so large that she can't move around. She has to be fed by nimble, normal-sized ants that tend to all her needs.

BEING GREAT IS NOT SO GREAT

You've probably seen ants, since they live in most parts of the world. The ants you see running around have normal insect bodies, with three body segments and six legs. They can move quickly for their size. But the ants you see are only those that venture outside the ant nest or colony. Inside, the great bulbous body of the queen lies surrounded by attendants who bring her food, clean away her waste, and carry off the eggs she lays to where they can develop into ants. She just blobs around all day, never going anywhere (she's too heavy to move herself) or doing anything.

Fast Facts

Name: Carpenter ant (queen), many types
Size: Up to 2 cm (0.8 in) long
Home: Forests around most of the world, wooden structures
Eats: Dead insects, nectar, and other sweet liquids

ANTISOCIAL

Ants, termites, bees, and hornets are social animals. This means that they live in large colonies and work together. Individuals are born to take on different roles, and they can't just swap jobs if they don't like them.

Some are workers, some are soldiers, some bees are drones, and there's always a queen, whose job is reproduction. They don't have lives as individuals, but the whole colony acts together like a super-organism.

SIPHONOPHORES ARE A COLONY OF CLONES

Siphonophores are animals that live in the sea—or maybe they're colonies that live in the sea. A siphonophore acts like a single organism, yet it's made up of hundreds or thousands of small creatures called zooids (say "zoo-oyd"). Somehow, these cooperate to act as one being.

TUBES AND BLOBS

Some siphonophores look like huge tubes. They grow to 2–3 m (6 ft 7 in–9 ft 10 in) long, are hollow on the inside, and have rubbery walls. Most are long, thin, strands. Some seem to have tentacles or are decorated with knobbly bits or tendrils. They can move, digest food, reproduce, and so on just like a single organism.

Just stringing along!

Their bodies are made up of different types of zooids, which are adapted to different tasks. Some are in charge of jet propulsion, bringing in water and then spurting it out at speed to move the siphonophore forward. Others are responsible for buoyancy, keeping the colony at the right point in the water between floating and sinking.

DEADLY BUT SLOPPY

If you saw a Portuguese man-of-war in the sea, you'd think that it was a jellyfish, since it looks like one. This siphonophore colony makes a bulb at the top and a set of streaming tentacles. It functions just like a jellyfish, with stinging tentacles to kill animals it can eat. Like jellyfish, many siphonophores are carnivores. They trail tentacles covered with stinging cells in the water, then wrap them around prey before shooting poisonous stings into the unfortunate animal.

Fast Facts

Name: Portuguese man-of-war
Size: Bladder (floating part) up to 30 cm (12 in) long, tentacles 10–30 m (33–100 ft) long
Home: Surface of the water in warm and tropical seas
Eats: Small fish, crustaceans (such as shrimp)

A PEA CRAB LIVES IN A SEA CUCUMBER'S BOTTOM

A pea crab is a tiny crab that lives inside another animal—often a shellfish, such as an oyster, a sea cucumber, or a sea urchin. A sea cucumber looks like a large leathery slug and lives on the ocean floor. Clearly, it has a nice bottom ... at least if you're a pea crab!

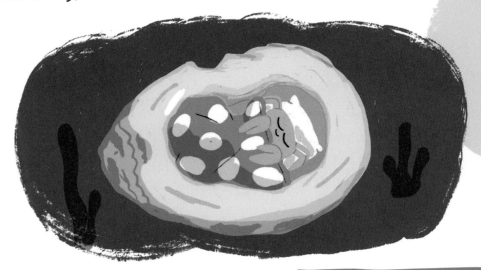

A THIEF IN THE HOUSE

Living inside the sea cucumber or other sea animal, the pea crab is a parasite. This means that it takes something from its host—such as food or a living space, or both—but gives nothing back in return. The pea crab is living rent-free in the sea cucumber's anus and stealing food from it—though likely food that isn't wanted anyway, since it's on the way out.

Fast Facts

Name: Pea crab
Size: 1.2 cm (0.5 in) across
Home: Inside a shellfish or other sea animal
Eats: Food stolen from the animal it lives inside.

There are many different types of parasites in the animal kingdom. Some are tiny (such as the pea crab, fleas, and lice) and some can be very big. Some types of tapeworms, which live in the guts of other animals, can grow to 10 m (33 ft) or longer. Some parasites eat food their host has eaten, and others feed on the host's body.

ONE AFTER ANOTHER

Some parasites stay in the same host for their whole life, but others move through different types of animals. Some tapeworms, for example, live in a mammal's gut as adults, and release eggs that come out in poop. In water or on the grass, the eggs hatch into larvae that are eaten by tiny animals. These are eaten in turn by a larger animal, and the larvae develop into worms inside them.

VAMPIRE BATS SHARE MEALS OF BLOOD

Vampire bats feed on the blood of other animals, often cattle. If a bat can't find a meal, it's in danger of starvation. Luckily, the bats live in large colonies, and another bat will often share its meal. That's not as easy as it sounds. The bats don't take a cup and fill it with blood! To share a meal, the bat has to vomit up the blood it has eaten. Appetizing? Maybe if you're a bat it is.

SHARE AND SHARE ALIKE

Scientists think that animals which help each other in the way vampire bats do are forming strong social bonds that benefit individuals and help the whole colony to survive. A bat which has been given a meal of blood-vomit is more likely to do the same for another hungry bat.

Fast Facts

Name: Vampire bat
Size: 9 cm (3.5 in) long, wingspan 18 cm (7 in)
Home: Mexico, Central and South America, Caribbean
Eats: Blood

Bats also seem to test the water. In a new group, they start by offering other services to each other, such as grooming. If the kindness is returned, the bats are more likely to share food later.

KINDLY RATS

Not all animals help others in the hope of a reward. Being helpful or generous without hoping to benefit, and at some cost or risk, is called altruism. There is more and more evidence of animals being altruistic. A laboratory rat will free a trapped rat even if that means that it has to share its own food.

Some animals even help those of different species. There are many stories of dolphins keeping drowning people afloat, and humpback whales have been seen saving seals from orcas that want to eat them!

ELECTRIC EELS SPIT IN THEIR NEST

More precisely, they spit to make their nest. The daddy electric eel forms the nest from bubbles of his own saliva. You can imagine that it would be quite hard to make a nest underwater from spit. The bubbles of spit are filled with air, so that they rise to the surface, making a floating nest.

FROTHY HOME

After the male eel has fashioned a frothy bubble-nest, the female lays up to 1,200 eggs. The male guards the nest until the eggs hatch a week later. Then his real work starts, since he has to keep the nest in good repair and catch and return any escaping babies until they're big enough to look after themselves. It's quite easy to repair the nest—he just needs to spit more bubbles. But since the mother keeps laying more eggs, he can be looking after eggs, new babies, and older babies all at once. It must be quite a challenging task.

SPITTING BIRDS

Electric eels aren't the only animals to make a nest from spit. Some other fish and some frogs do it, too. And the most famous spitters are swiftlets—small birds that live in caves. The swiftlets construct their nest from strands of saliva that harden on contact with the air. The nest is made in a cup-shape attached to the roof of a cave. Sadly, people harvest the nests to make soup (yes, bird-spit soup), so the number of swiftlets is falling.

GIANT TUBE WORMS DON'T EAT ANYTHING

They also thrive in dangerously hot, poisonous water and might live for hundreds of years. They sound like something from another planet, but they live deep in Earth's oceans.

WORM WITH A SHELL

Worms are usually soft and wiggle through soil or wherever they live. Tube worms, though, build themselves a hard, tubelike shell fixed to a rock, and they can't move anywhere else. They live in huge colonies in the deepest seas, up to 3.6 km (2.2 mi) down, where the pressure is immense and it's completely dark all the time. They attach themselves to hydrothermal vents, which are undersea volcanoes that belch out scorching hot water full of acid—not the nicest living space!

NO MOUTH, NO FOOD

A tube worm doesn't have a mouth or stomach. Instead, bacteria inside it process chemicals in the water to make sugars, which the tube worm uses. The chemicals are toxic sulfides from the hydrothermal vent.

Nothing for you!

What's for dinner?

Fast Facts

Name: Giant tube worm
Size: Up to 3 m (9 ft 10 in) long, 4 cm (1.6 in) across
Home: Hydrothermal vents in the Pacific Ocean
Eats: Chemicals from seawater

LIFE WITHOUT THE SUN

Unlike almost all other life on Earth, tube worms don't rely on energy from the Sun for their food. Elsewhere, plants use sunlight to produce leaves, fruit, and so on, which animals eat, either directly or by eating other animals. Or tiny algae use sunlight to grow, and are eaten. The worms of the hydrothermal vent don't rely on sunlight at all, but live only on chemicals from within Earth. They give scientists clues about how things might possibly survive on other planets or moons that are too far from their star for its heat to be of much use.

AFRICAN ASSASSIN BUGS CARRY THEIR DEAD VICTIMS AROUND

As its name suggests, an assassin bug kills things. But it doesn't just eat them and leave the leftovers behind. Instead, a type of assassin bug from Africa sucks out all the tasty bits, then carries the empty outer covering around on its back, glued to the remains of previous meals.

THE WALKING DEAD

An assassin bug often looks like a pile of ants stuck together—but they are all dead, yet moving. The bug stabs its proboscis (long, sharp mouth part) into its victim and injects it with saliva which contains chemicals that both paralyze the victim and dissolve its body tissues. Then it sucks the insect soup back up, leaving the crispy outside. Next, it makes sticky stuff to glue the dead insect to the pile on its back. It can carry up to 20 ants, making a heap bigger than itself. To any possible predator, it doesn't look at all like a tasty assassin beetle. It looks like an uncanny pile of ant zombies. That should be enough to put most things off eating it.

LOOK WHAT I'M NOT

Animals disguising themselves as something they are not is called mimicry. Some do it to avoid being eaten, while others do it to enable them to catch animals they want to eat. Some insects have evolved to look like leaves or twigs so that they're hard to spot, and hungry predators overlook them. The orchid mantis looks like an orchid flower and eats insects that are fooled into landing on it. Not many animals try to look like a pile of ants, though.

Fast Facts

Name: Assassin bug
Size: 1 cm (0.4 in) long
Home: Grasslands of East
   Africa
Eats: Insects

AXOLOTLS ARE BIG BABIES

Axolotls are amphibians related to salamanders. But unlike salamanders, axolotls never grow up. Salamanders start off as babies living in the water and then change their bodies to live on land as adults, whereas axolotls stay the same and remain in the water. They just get bigger!

WET OR DRY?

Amphibians rely on water, but usually the adults breathe air and live on land. All amphibians lay their eggs in water. The eggs are soft and sloppy, and would quickly dry out in air. The young that hatch from the eggs are larvae—an immature form of the animal that will change as it grows. You've probably seen tadpoles, which are the larvae of frogs. Other amphibians also start as larvae that don't look like their parents and which live in the water all the time. Amphibian larvae have gills to breathe in water.

Fast Facts

Name: Axolotl
Size: 23–30 cm (9-12 in) long
Home: Lakes Xochimilco and Chalco in the Valley of Mexico
Eats: Worms, insects, other arthropods, small fish

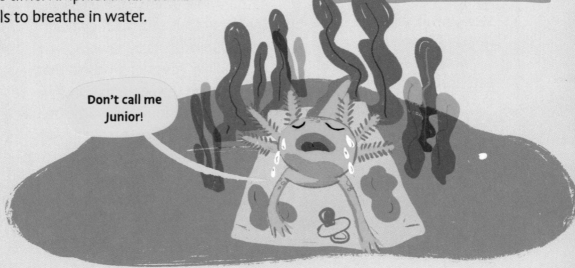

Don't call me Junior!

ALL CHANGE!

Over time, most larvae change, going through a process called metamorphosis. Tadpoles grow legs and lose their tails, changing from animals that swim to ones that walk or jump on land. As tadpoles, they have gills—feathery structures on either side of the head which take oxygen from the water. As adult frogs or toads, they lose their gills and have lungs for breathing air, just like you.

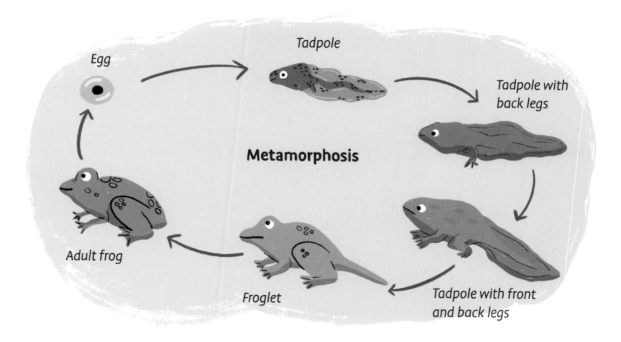

Egg

Tadpole

Tadpole with back legs

Metamorphosis

Adult frog

Froglet

Tadpole with front and back legs

FOREVER YOUNG

Axolotls stay in the larval stage. They grow legs but they don't lose their gills. They need to stay in water nearly all the time. But unlike most larval forms, they can reproduce. After a year, they're ready to lay eggs and have their own babies.

ALASKAN FROGS CAN BE FROZEN SOLID

It gets very cold in Alaska, so it's not a great place to be a cold-blooded frog that can't control its own temperature. Without the ability to keep its body warm, a frog in Alaska can actually freeze. Indeed, it freezes nearly solid. If you bent one of its legs (don't!), it would snap. Freezing kills most animals, but not Alaskan frogs.

ICE-FREE ZONE

Animals have different ways of dealing with conditions that are uncomfortably hot or cold. Some fish that live in Arctic and Antarctic seas have antifreeze in their blood. This acts in the same way as the antifreeze people sometimes put in their cars in winter. The molecules (tiny particles) of antifreeze get in between the molecules of water, preventing them from forming bonds to make ice.

Fast Facts

Name: Alaskan wood frog
Size: 3.5–7.5 cm (1.4–3 in) long
Home: Canada, Alaska
Eats: Spiders, beetles, slugs, snails, decaying plants and animal bodies, eggs and larvae of amphibians

TOUGHING IT OUT

Alaskan wood frogs, though, don't have antifreeze—they just let their bodies freeze. When this happens, they are nearly dead—the heart stops beating, the frog doesn't breathe, and blood doesn't flow. The frogs can stay frozen for seven months and when spring comes, they defrost and hop away.

Ah, the frozen-food section!

GETTING READY

It seems that each individual cell of the frog keeps doing what is needed so the frog doesn't die, but the organism as a whole does nothing. In preparation, the frog freezes overnight and thaws in the daytime when it's warm enough. Repeating this process gives the frog time to collect the glucose (sugar) it needs in its cells, ready for the marathon cold spell. With enough glucose to keep its cells working normally, the frog can avoid freezing to death while it waits for warmer weather.

MOURNING GECKOS ARE NEARLY ALL FEMALE

We mostly tend to think of animals as being either male or female, with about the same number of each in the natural world. But it's not that simple. Most mourning geckos are female. Other animals might start out one sex and change, or their sex depends on the conditions where they live.

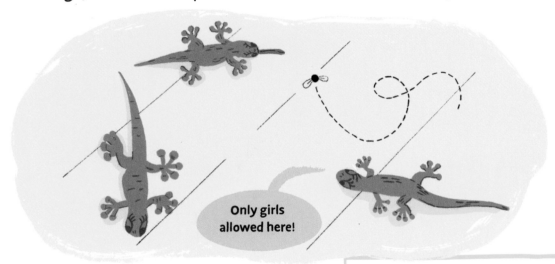

Only girls allowed here!

ALL THE SINGLE LADIES

Mourning geckos live around the coasts of the Indian and Pacific Oceans. Almost all of them are female. They reproduce by a process called parthenogenesis, which means that the babies hatch from unfertilized eggs. The babies are clones (exact copies) of the mother. Occasionally, a boy gecko hatches, but they're usually infertile (can't reproduce).

Fast Facts

Name: Mourning gecko
Size: Up to 10 cm (4 in) long
Home: Coasts of Indian and Pacific Oceans, and in South America
Eats: Insects, spiders, fruit, pollen, nectar

UNDECIDED

Clownfish are bright orange-and-white striped fish. People often say all clownfish are born male, but actually they're born with both male and female reproductive organs. As the fish grow older, two in a group become larger. They develop into a male and a female. That pair reproduces, while all the small fish become male and don't reproduce. If the large female is lost or dies, the large male changes sex to become female, and one of the small males grows bigger and takes over as the only daddy fish.

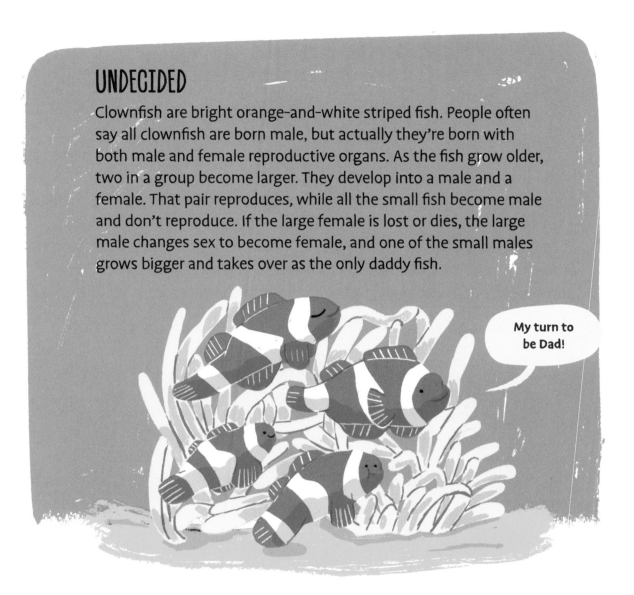

My turn to be Dad!

HOT OR COLD?

The embryo inside a reptile egg can turn into a male or a female. Which it will be depends on the temperature. For tortoises, cool temperatures lead to male babies, and warmer temperatures to female babies. For crocodiles and snapping turtles, hot or cold temperatures produce females, and in-between temperatures produce males.

SURINAM TOADS HATCH OUT OF THEIR MOTHERS' BACKS

Most animals that lay eggs either put them in a nest or leave them somewhere to hatch alone, but the Surinam toad does things differently. After the mother has laid the eggs, the dad moves them onto her back. There, a layer of skin grows over the eggs, keeping them safe. After four or five months, they push their way out through holes in the skin. They don't come out as tadpoles, but as fully formed tiny toadlets.

I got you under my skin!

CAREFUL PARENTS

The Surinam toad's babies are safe under the mother's skin—they'll only get eaten if she's eaten. Some types of fish even keep their eggs or babies in their mouths. It can be the mother or the father that looks after the eggs, depending on the type of fish. Most can't eat while they have eggs in their mouths, so they are thin and hungry by the time the babies come out.

Fast Facts

Name: Common Surinam toad
Size: 16 cm (6.5 in) long
Home: Northern South
America
Eats: Worms, insects, small
fish, crustaceans

Seahorses are strange-looking fish with a head rather like a horse's head. They're unusual in that the dad gives birth! He has a special pouch on his body where the female puts her eggs. They are fertilized in the pouch and the babies grow inside the eggs until they hatch. Then they pop out of the dad's pouch and swim off to live on their own.

GLOSSARY

ABDOMEN Main part of an animal's body, below the head.

ALGAE (SINGULAR ALGA) Tiny organisms that make their food using energy from sunlight. Most live in water.

ANCESTOR A parent, grandparent or other previous relative in a direct line of descent.

BACTERIA Tiny organisms with one cell that are too small to see without a microscope.

BULBOUS Fat and rounded, bulb-shaped.

CARBON DATING Process of working out the approximate age of something by comparing different types of the element carbon that are found in it.

CELL Building block of living things; all organisms are made of at least one cell.

COOPERATE Work together.

DEHYDRATED Dried out.

DIAGNOSIS Identification of what it is wrong with someone who is unwell.

DIFFERENTIATE Divide into different types.

DIGESTION The process of breaking down food and absorbing useful chemicals from it.

ECHIDNA A spiny anteater from Australia and New Guinea that lays eggs.

ELECTROMAGNETIC SPECTRUM The range of types of energy that travel as waves, from radio waves to gamma rays.

ENDANGERED Threatened with dying out.

EPILEPSY A brain condition that causes sudden bursts of electricity in the brain, resulting in seizures or fits.

EVAPORATE Turn from liquid to gas.

EVOLUTION The process of a species (type) of organism changing over time, often adapting to changes in its living conditions.

EXTENSION An extra bit.

FERTILIZE Make ready to grow.

GENERATE Produce.

GROOM In animals, tend to the fur of another, often picking out parasites.

HIBERNATE Reduce body processes and sleep through the winter.

ILLUMINATED Lit up.

IMMORTAL Living forever

ISOLATED Stranded alone.

KRILL Small shrimp-like animals found in large numbers in the sea.

LANDMINE Explosive device hidden underground as a weapon.

LARVAE Singular larva) immature form of an animal that will change as it grows.

LIVESTOCK Animals kept for food.

LOBE Fleshy rounded part of a body.

LURE Something intended to attract another organism.

METABOLIC RATE The rate at which an animal's body works and its biological processes work.

MOLLUSK A type of animal that has no bones, a soft body, and often has a hard shell.

NOURISHMENT
Food.

NUTRIENT
Chemical from food
that is useful to
the body.

NUTRITIOUS
Health-giving.

ORGAN Structure in
the body that
carries out a
particular function,
such as the lungs
used for breathing
or the heart for
pumping blood.

OXYGEN A gas in
the air which all
animals need
to breathe.

PARALYSE Make
incapable of
moving.

PECTORAL (FIN)
Fin near the front
of a fish that comes
from the area that
became the shoulder
in land animals.

PIGMENT Chemical
which gives a
substance its hue.

PLANKTON Tiny
organisms that live
in water and are too
small to see without
a microscope.

PLANULA An
early stage in the
development of
a jellyfish.

POLLEN A
powedery
substance produced
by flowers that
contain the male
cells needed for
reproduction.

POLYP A stage in
the development of
a jellyfish which
attaches to a
surface after the
planula settles. It is
secured with a foot
at the bottom and
has tentacles
around a mouth at
the top of a stalk.

PREDATOR An
animal that hunts
and eats other
animals.

PROTEIN A type of
chemical essential
to the growing and
working of living
bodies.

QUADRUPLET One
of a set of four
identical babies.

RADIATION Energy
that travels in the
form of waves
through space and
matter.

REHYDRATE Add
water to something
that has dried out.

REPRODUCE
Produce offspring.

SCUTE A panel on
the shell of a tortoise.

SEIZURE An episode
of sudden electrical
activity in the brain
that can causes
someone's muscles
to jerk.

SPERM Male cell
that must combine
with a female egg
cell to start a new
baby animal.

STRATEGY A plan
of action.

SULFIDE A chemical
containing sulfur
often found near
volcanoes.

TALON Claw

TEAT The nipple
through which baby
mammals are
provided with milk.

TENDRIL Long
strand.

TISSUE A collection
of similar cells in an
organism, such as
skin or muscle.

TOXIC Poisonous.

URINE Wee.

VACUUM Space
containing no
matter.

VOLCANIC Relating
to volcanoes, areas
where hot molten
rock rises to the
surface of Earth.

VULNERABLE Easily
harmed.

WAVELENGTH The
distance between
two wave peaks; the
wavelength of
electromagnetic
radiation sets how
the energy behaves
— as light, radio,
microwaves, and
so on.

INDEX